GATES OF THE GROVE

KIDS' SHABBAT ON THE BEACH

*In honor of our grandchildren Abigail & Rebecca Salzhauer
Daryl & Steve Roth*

Rabbi David J. Gelfand   Rabbi Alon Levkovitz
Donald Zucker, President   Cantor Debra Stein

THE JEWISH CENTER OF THE HAMPTONS
44 WOODS LANE, PO BOX 5107, EAST HAMPTON, NY 11937 (631) 324-9858
www.jcoh.org

Let's Talk About God

Dorothy K. Kripke

illustrated by Christine Tripp

Library of Congress Cataloging-in-Publication Data

Kripke, Dorothy Karp.

Let's talk about God / Dorothy K. Kripke ; illustrated by Christine Tripp

  p. cm.

 Summary: An introduction to the nature, characteristics, and actions of God, as well as God's relationship with people.

 ISBN #1-881283-34-8

  1. God (Judaism)—Juvenile literature. [1. God (Judaism)] I. Tripp, Christine, ill. II. Title

BM610.k7 2003

296.3'11

2003052283

Alef Design Group• 4423 Fruitland Avenue, Los Angeles, CA 90058
(800) 845-0662 • (323) 582-1200 • fax (323) 585–0327
Website WWW.ALEFDESIGN.COM

MANUFACTURED IN CHINA

CONTENTS

ONE GOD

God is not a person,
Or moon, or stars, or sun.
God is the good that's in the world,
And God is only One.

God is not a person,
and not a great big king.
God is the good that's in the world,
And God made everything.

4

Long, long ago people did not know about God.

Some saw the bright, warm sun in the sky, and they said, "The sun must be God."

Some saw their king, who was very mighty, and they said, "The king must be God."

People said, "There are many gods. There are tree gods, and river gods, and mountain gods." But a man named Abraham said, "No, there is only one God. God made the trees and the rivers and the mountains and the sun and the kings. God made all of us, too."

Abraham said, "There is only one God. God is the God of all the world. But we cannot see God. God is the goodness that is in the world.

Abraham lived long ago. He was the father of the Jewish people. He was the first man to know that there is only one God and that God loves all the people in the world. Abraham was the first to know that one God made the whole world.

There is only one God. But God has many names. Sometimes we call God a ruler and sometimes we call God a parent. Just as your parents love you and take care of you and help you, God loves all the people in the world. God takes care of us all and helps us all. That is why we call God our Heavenly Parent. God has other names too, but there is only one God.

GOD MADE THE WORLD

The crunchy earth,
The blue-white sky,
Green things that grow,
The sun on high,
The fish and beasts
And birds that fly,
God made these and
The world began.
And last of all,
God made a Man.

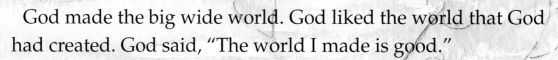

God made the big wide world. God liked the world that God had created. God said, "The world I made is good."

Then God made the blue sky and liked it too. God said, "The sky I made is good."

Next God made the green grass and the tall trees and gay sweet-smelling flowers and all growing things. God liked the growing things. God said, "The growing things I made are good."

After that God made the bright sun to give light to the world by day, and the silver moon to give light at night. God liked the sun and moon and said, "The sun and moon are good."

Then God made living things for the world— swimming fish for the seas, flying birds for the sky, and swift animals for the earth. God said, "The living things I made are good."

Last of all, God made people. God put a little of piece of God into people, to make them special and different from all other living things. God was pleased with people and God said, "People are good."

When God finished all the work, God rested. God liked the resting and said, "People must rest too. People may work for six days, but on the seventh day, everyone must rest. It is good to rest." That is why we have the Sabbath, a special day for rest and prayer and fun with family and friends.

GOD IS EVERYWHERE

We know that God is always there,
'Round about us
Everywhere.

God is everywhere all the time.

People and things can be in only one place at one time. If you are in the house, you are not in your backyard. If you are in your backyard, you are not in the house.

But God is different. God is everywhere all the time. God is outdoors and at the same time God is in every room in your house. And God is also in all the houses, everywhere. Just as air is all around us, so God is everywhere all the time.

It makes us feel safe to know that wherever we go, God is with us. And at the same time God is with all the other people in the world. God is *in* all the people in the world, too, because when God made people, God put a little piece of God into each one.

Only God can be everywhere all the time. Only God was, and is, and will be, everywhere. That is because God is so very wonderful.

WE CANNOT SEE GOD

God is never seen,
And yet we know that God is there,
Because we see the things God does
And feel God's loving care.

    We cannot see God. We know God is all around us all the time, but God cannot be seen.

    We cannot see many things. We cannot see the wind. But we see autumn leaves flying and dancing, all orange and gold. We see a bright green kite sailing in the sky. Then we know the wind is there. We see what the wind does, even though we cannot see the wind itself.

We cannot see love, but we know when someone loves us. We feel love in a hug or a smile or a friendly look or a warm touch. We feel love in many ways, but we never see love. We know it by what it does to us. Love makes us feel good inside. It makes us feel safe and happy. It makes us love other people, and it makes us pleased with ourselves. We know what love does for us, but we cannot see love.

We cannot see God. But we do see what God does in the world. We know God is everywhere all around us. We cannot see God, but we know that God is there.

THINGS GOD GIVES US

Our ears can hear,
Our eyes can see.
Our noses are made for smell.
Our hands can touch,
Our tongues can taste.
God planned us very well.

14

God gives us many things. God gives us wonderful bodies, so that we can walk and run and hear and see and touch and smell and taste.

God gives us food so that we can eat and grow strong.

God gives us sleep so that we can rest.

God gives us teachers to help us learn things.

God gives us friends to share our play and our thoughts—and sometimes even our sadness.

God gives children to people to make people happy.

God gives us love and happiness.

God gives us puppies and butterflies and brooks and flowers and rainbows and snowflakes. God gives us the warm sun and the twinkling stars. God gives us the chirping of birds, the humming of crickets, the patter of rain, the answer of echoes. God gives us a good, big world with wonderful things in it.

15

GOD HELPS US

God helps to make us brave
and helps to keep us well.
God helps us in so many ways,
Much more than we can tell.

God does many things for us. When we are sick, God helps us to get well again. God helps our bodies fight the germs that make us sick. The doctor's medicine fights the germs, and we fight the germs. Soon we are out of bed and well again.

Sometimes there are things that make us unhappy. If we remember that God is good and will help us—especially if we try hard to help ourselves—then we feel brave. And when we are brave, we can do wonderful things. Remembering about God helps to make us brave.

If we are frightened because we are doing something new or going someplace new, God helps us. If we say, "I will be careful and God will help me, because God is right here with me," then we feel better. We are not frightened any more.

When we are sad or in trouble, God helps and comforts us. God finds a way to make things better. And soon they *are* better. God wants us to be happy because God is good.

GOD'S SPECIAL GIFTS

To think and speak are special gifts
God gives to you and me.
And that is why we all must try
To use them carefully.

When God made the world, God gave people a special gift, a brain with which to think and a tongue with which to speak.

It is wonderful that we can speak and tell each other things. Dogs can bark but they cannot speak and tell what they want. Ducks can quack but they cannot speak and tell what they want. Pigs grunt and cows moo but they cannot tell what they want. People are especially lucky to be able to speak and tell each other exactly what they want and think. Speech is a very precious gift from God.

It is also wonderful that we can think and know things. It is wonderful that we can remember some things and learn others. Learning is fun. It's fun to learn to read a book or bake a cake or build a boat.

Sometimes people get a special idea. God helps them get the idea and God helps them as they work on it. That is how beautiful stories and poems and pictures are made. And that is how wonderful things like rockets and computers and even new sneakers are invented.

God wants us to enjoy the world. That is why God gave us special gifts. And that is why we are able to make the world a better and happier place. God made us able to make ourselves better, and make the world better too.

GOD TELLS US WHAT TO DO

The Bible books
That God did give
Teach all people
How to live.

To all people,
Great and small,
The Bible teaches:
"Love them all."

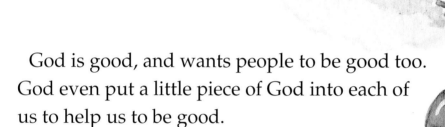

God is good, and wants people to be good too. God even put a little piece of God into each of us to help us to be good.

God gave us the Ten Commandments and the rest of the Bible. They tell us the good way to live. God said, "This is the good way. But I will not force you to be good. You must choose for yourself. If you choose to be good, you will be a little like Me, and you will be happy."

The Bible tells us: "Love your neighbor as yourself." Long ago a great Rabbi, Hillel, explained this. He said, "Do not do to anyone else what you would not want done to you." Another way of saying this is: "Treat other people the way you want them to treat you."

God wants us to love. God wants us to love our parents and teachers and friends. If we love them and help them, we are happy.

God wants us to be kind, and to share the things we have with other people. God is kind to us and shares the whole world with us. When we share our food and our toys and our treats and our fun, we are a little like God, and we are happy.

God wants us to love people. God loves all people. God doesn't care whether we are pretty or not, young or old, red-haired or black-haired, rich or poor, strong or weak. God loves us all, no matter who we are or how we look. God made us all and loves us all. God wants us to love all people no matter how different they are from us.

That is what the teachers of long ago meant when they told us that God wants people to be like God, helpful, kind, and full of love.

SOMETIMES WE MAKE MISTAKES

God and friends and parents
Forgive wrong things we do,
If we can say, "I'm sorry,"
And really mean it, too!

No one is perfect. People—all people—make mistakes sometimes. All people—even you and even I—do the wrong thing sometimes. And when we do the wrong thing, the little piece of God inside us says, "This is not good."

22

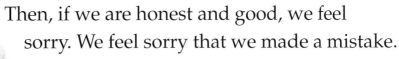

Then, if we are honest and good, we feel sorry. We feel sorry that we made a mistake. And we say to ourselves, "I will try to understand why I made this mistake. I will try never to make this same mistake again." If we do that, we can learn something very important from the mistakes we make.

When we hurt another person, Mother or Daddy or anybody at all, and we say, "I'm sorry," and really mean it too, that person feels better. Most of the hurt seems to go away. Then *we* feel better too.

Our mothers and fathers love us even when we make mistakes or do the wrong thing. Even though we sometimes do something wrong, God still loves us, too. And if we are really sorry, God forgives us too. God knows that no one is perfect.

23

HOW WE TALK TO GOD

We ask God to give us
All the things we need to live.
We thank God for kindly care.
All this we do in words of prayer.

There are times when people feel they want to talk to God. It is good for us to talk to God. When we talk to God, we call our talk "prayer."

Often we want to talk to God to say thank You. We thank God for our food. We thank God when we wake up to a bright new day. We thank God for our rest at night. We thank God for taking care of us. We say our thanks for the Sabbath and all the holidays. We say thank You for giving us the Bible and for teaching us how to live.

Sometimes when we talk to God, we ask for things— for important things. We ask God to keep us well and strong. We ask God to make us good. We ask God to give us a healthy and a happy year. We pray that there may be no wars, and that all the world may have peace.

When we talk to God, we ask God for some things and we thank God for others.

HOW GOD TALKS TO US

God's voice within
  our heart and mind
Tells us to be
  brave and kind.
If we but listen
  we can hear
The voice within us,
  sweet and clear.

Sometimes God talks to us too. God doesn't talk with a mouth or a voice, and yet God tells us things.

Have you ever wondered what to do about something? And then suddenly did you feel, "I know exactly what is right?" Perhaps it was the little bit of God inside you that told you what to do.

26

Have you ever done something very kind, like helping someone, or sharing your toys and treats? And did you feel good and warm and happy inside yourself? Couldn't you almost hear God inside you say, "I'm so proud of you"?

Have you ever been hurt and tried very hard to be brave? Didn't being brave help, and didn't it make you feel the pain a little less? And couldn't you almost hear God inside you saying, "I'm so very proud of you"?

God talks to us through ourselves and through other people too. A long time ago certain people felt that God had spoken to them, and so they wrote down God's words in books. These books are called the Bible. The Bible tells us how God wants us to live. That is why the Bible is so important and holy.

God talks to us through wonderful books like the Bible and through ourselves too.

27

GOD IS DIFFERENT FROM PEOPLE

God is not a person,
and God we cannot see.
God's not at all like us,
Yet like God we try to be.

God is different from people. All people forget sometimes and make mistakes sometimes. No one is perfect. But God is different from people. God never forgets and never makes mistakes. God is perfect.

People are *usually* good, but not *always* good. Sometimes we make a mistake and are not good. But God is different from people. God is always good.

People can be in only one place at a time. If you are at the seashore, you are not in the mountains. But God is different from people. God is everywhere all the time.

28

People can do some things and not others. You can ride a bicycle or tricycle, but you cannot drive an automobile. No one can do everything. But God is different from people. God can do everything.

People speak with their voices. When Mother is in the kitchen and you are outdoors, she has to call to you so you can hear her. God is different from people. God can speak in a still, small voice, or no voice at all, and still inside of us we hear God.

People get tired and need to sleep. God is different from people. God is never tired and never sleeps.

People grow and change. Once you were a tiny baby, but now you are getting big. The shoes you wore last year are too small for you now. You are changing all the time. But God is different from people. God is not a person and never changes. God is always the same.

God is very different from people in many ways. God is not a person at all.

There are some things we don't know about the world. We don't know why it is that birds can fly high in the sky—and fish can live in the sea. We don't know why some flowers are red and others are yellow. There are some things we don't know about the world.

There are many things we don't know about God. There are many questions no one can answer, not parents, not teachers, not rabbis. There are some things nobody knows but God alone.

But it doesn't matter that we don't know everything about God. It is much more important that we know how God wants us to live. And we do know that, because the Torah tells us and our parents tell us. And the little bit of God inside each one of us tells us, too.

There are many things we *do* know about God. We know there is one God in the world, and that God is good and loves us. We know that God takes care of us and helps us. We know that God made the world and is everywhere in it. We know that God made us and taught us how to live. There are many things we know about God.

It really doesn't matter that we don't know *everything* about God. The important thing is for us to be good and kind and helpful to other people, just as God is good and kind and helpful to us.

God is One and God is the only God. The more we love each other and all the people God created, the more we show our love of God.

It isn't so important and
It isn't even odd
That we don't know so many things
About the ways of God.

The thing that matters most of all
We're very certain of:
That God told people we must live
In friendship and in love.